*Quick*GUIDES
everything you need to know...fast

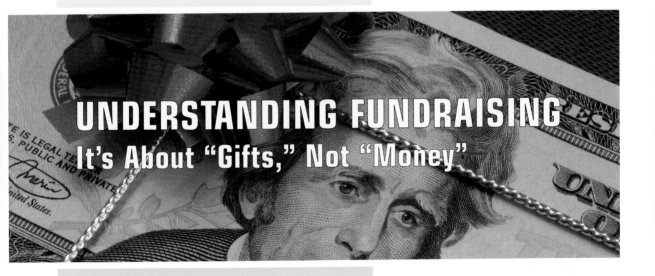

UNDERSTANDING FUNDRAISING
It's About "Gifts," Not "Money"

by **Adrienne Hall**

reviewed by Gerlinde Scholz

WIREMILL
PUBLISHING LTD

Across the world the organizations and institutions that fundraise to finance their work are referred to in many different ways. They are charities, non-profits or not-for-profit organizations, non-governmental organizations (NGOs), voluntary organizations, academic institutions, agencies, etc. For ease of reading, we have used the term Nonprofit Organization, Organization or NPO as an umbrella term throughout the *Quick*Guide series. We have also used the spellings and punctuation used by the author.

Published by
Wiremill Publishing Ltd.
Edenbridge, Kent TN8 5PS, UK
info@wiremillpublishing.com
www.wiremillpublishing.com
www.quickguidesonline.com

British Library Cataloguing in Publication Data
A catalogue record for this book is available from the British Library.

ISBN Number 1-905053-17-7

Printed by Rhythm Consolidated Berhad, Malaysia
Cover Design by Jennie de Lima and Edward Way
Design by Colin Woodman Design

CONTENTS

UNDERSTANDING FUNDRAISING
IT'S ABOUT "GIFTS," NOT "MONEY"

INTRODUCTION: SETTING THE SCENE

This Guide is to assist people in nonprofit organisations (NPOs) who are considering a fundraising programme as well as those already involved in fundraising who would benefit from a review of an existing programme. It seeks to demystify the fundraising process and to provide an introduction within development and philanthropy to help NPOs plan and link short-term activities with long-term strategies.

This relationship is illustrated in a simple diagram developed by Robert Payton.

Values-Based Philanthropy, Development and Fundraising

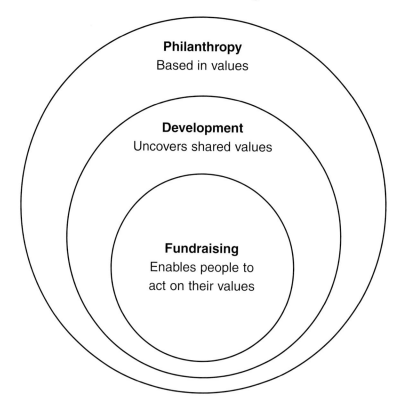

Philanthropy
Based in values

Development
Uncovers shared values

Fundraising
Enables people to
act on their values

INTRODUCTION: SETTING THE SCENE

At the centre of this process are core values that are understood and shared. These core values need to be clearly articulated. No one belongs to, works for, gives to, or associates with an organisation that doesn't share his or her values. Fundraising takes place in the context of philanthropy, and people engage in philanthropy for complex reasons. Ego, fear, guilt, and power can all play a part. But at some point, the uniting factor becomes a sharing of values: the belief that an organisation is providing a service which not only adds value but also is capable of transforming society, and without which society and the quality of individual and collective life would be diminished. Development is the activity that marries the organisation's values with its potential supporters. Fundraising enables prospects to act on their values by investing in various ways. These might include legacies, memberships, annual gifts, capital gifts, volunteering, and event participation; all of these will be touched on in this Guide but explained in more detail in other titles in the *Quick*Guide series.

Nonprofit organisations need money for their operating costs and to fund programmes and activities that, as a result, benefit society. To maximise fundraising returns, it is important to think about the process and its context, the words you use to describe what you do, and the way you plan and implement your fundraising programme.

To do this, you must understand the relationship between money and gifts and recognise that money only becomes yours when an *individual* – whether acting alone or in a corporation, trust or foundation or public funding body – *chooses* to give it to you. Money only becomes yours when the donor makes a value judgment in your favour. Similarly, a donor's money only becomes a gift when you accept it. That acceptance is a step along a two-way street. Your organisation's credibility becomes closely linked with that of the donor when you enter into a gift relationship. To accept gifts from dubious sources is to risk your own organisation's credibility; conversely, association with

high-quality donors advances the standing of both parties.

Organisations that raise funds seek and accept gifts. A gift is more than just money: it represents money plus choice (yours and your donor's), so putting the donor in the centre of the process is the most important step you can take to ensure your programme's success.

In the same way that truly professional marketing puts the customer at the centre of the business process, development puts the donor and donor values, not money, in the centre of the fundraising process. Build good relationships with your "target markets" and profitable transactions will follow. Your aim should be to build strong, sustainable, long-term relationships with donors, not to get money through the door as fast as you can.

The diagram opposite illustrates the "virtuous circle" of investment in charities.

Focus of Development Activity

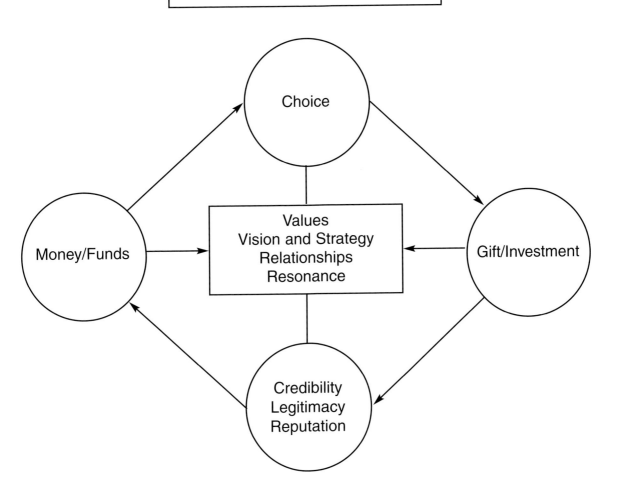

G iven the pressures of delivery in a competitive environment, it's easy to lose sight of one important fact. People don't give you money because you *have* needs but because you *meet* needs. Your first and most important task, then, is to define which needs you're meeting.

No matter whether your programme is social or economic welfare, education, the arts or whatever, it's vital to define *where* your organisation is and where it's going, *what* it stands for, and *how* it conducts its business.

Nonprofits compete with one another for donor investment. Central to the process of encouraging support of your organisation rather than another is to communicate clearly and precisely what makes your organisation and its contribution distinctive (in advertising "speak," your USP – unique selling point). You need to encourage and impart a sense of shared values, and not force, coerce or embarrass others into participation.

YOUR ORGANISATION'S ASPIRATIONS

Before you embark on your fundraising programme, or when reviewing an existing operation, it's important to identify those aspects of your organisation that make up your aspirations. These define the reason you will receive and accept gifts (your case for support).

The first of these is *vision.* Vision is the "big picture" image of what your organisation and, thus, your fundraising initiative are designed to achieve. Perhaps it's a world without hunger, without HIV/AIDS or without cancer. It may be providing rehabilitation to those who are disabled or reducing infant mortality in Africa. Whatever it is, it should be broad enough to encompass and express a focused vision of your organisation's objectives (concentrating on HIV/AIDS in a particular region or area, targeting a certain type of cancer or disability).

The second is your *mission.* Your mission must articulate why your organisation exists and, more importantly, what makes its contribution distinctive. There are sure to be many other organisations working in areas similar to yours (education, arts, welfare, environment, health), so the way in which you define and articulate your organisation's special "edge" within those broad parameters is critical to your success.

Thirdly, *organisational values* show how your organisation conducts itself in achieving its mission. Make sure you express them clearly and succinctly. Take hints from the business world and the way leading companies explain their values to their public. Most people can recall the most famous slogans, simply because they are so clear and memorable. A single sentence or phrase which sums up your organisation will help people inside and outside the organisation focus their minds on the way you do business.

Finally, think of your *strategy.* Remember the adage that if you don't know where you're going, any road will take you there. Your strategy is a road map taking you from where you are to where you want to be. It will show prospects and donors how their contribution can make, will make, or is making a difference in moving your organisation *and communities* forward.

You've defined your aspirations. Now you need to support your aspirations by identifying your funding prospects and their potential interest in your organisation. The way you acquire and manage this information will determine how successful you are, and also ensure that you maximise your limited resources. In this context, look at the following main areas.

First, remember the maxim that "time spent in reconnaissance is never wasted" and exhaustively **research** your "market," that is, the range of potential donors. Understanding them is crucial to success.

Reviewer's Comment
Giving is determined by a prospective supporter's capacity to give and his or her inclination to give. Both of those can be researched. Fundraising strategy focuses on working with prospects who are financially able to make a difference, to strengthen their inclination to give at the highest level possible.

To implement special and major gift programmes, you must identify those prospects capable of five-, six- and seven-figure gifts and, more importantly, you must be able to acquaint them with your activities to the point where they will make gifts at this level. The quality of your research – not only about their assets and personal circumstances, where appropriate, but also about their values and general philanthropic activities – will determine how well you do this.

Secondly, **profile** your broader universe which consists of all the potential stakeholders in your organisation – those people who would benefit from the success of your organisation and who share your values and objectives.

Thirdly, pay attention to your **database** and the way you store and manipulate information about your potential donors and stakeholders.

Reviewer's Comment
A database is not just a powerful operational tool. It provides essential management information and is a major factor in establishing your organisation's professionalism and credibility.

Database capacity and technical and staffing support will determine how well you optimise your resources, how effectively you plan and track your fundraising and demonstrate general management effectiveness.

A good database should be able to hold, search and manipulate all relevant data on potential and actual donors. As a basic requirement, it should include as much of the following information on individuals as possible:

- Contact details (names, home or business addresses, telephone/fax numbers and email addresses).

- Family information and a history of any family member's involvement with your organisation. (If you are dealing with a company, public organisation, trust or foundation, holding this information about the individual people you deal with is essential.)

- Career history.

- Business status and interests. Whether an individual is an entrepreneur or a corporate employee is important to the approach to giving and to their expectations.

- Educational background.

- Networks (club memberships, professional associations, business directorships, and so on).

- Where possible, financial information such as salary, investments, tangible assets, directors' fees, stocks, capital assets, estimated cash flow (for public corporations, such information is readily available through statutory documents).

- Donation history with your organisation and others.

- The prospect's response to previous direct-marketing initiatives, such as mailings, events and other contacts.

- Prospect tracking: your plans for the prospect and action prompts.

- Information about the prospect's values, interests and attitudes.

Continues on next page

Reviewer's Comment

In most countries, this kind of information is publicly available about companies, government agencies and funding bodies, and trusts and foundations. For individuals, such details are often protected by privacy or data protection legislation. It is your responsibility as a development professional to be familiar with the relevant laws that apply in your country and to ensure that your prospect research and data management fully comply with those laws. A breach of privacy regulations by an NPO has potential to cause serious damage to reputation and loss of donor confidence.

Fourthly, consider **budgets and financial planning** for your fundraising operation. Leveraging is the process of maximising the ratio between an investment and its return. It is as important to NPOs as it is to profit-seeking ventures, and you need to work hard at it. Investors – in your case, donors – need the assurance that your organisation is putting its resources into end-user programmes rather than operations, management and promotions. Hence, investment in fundraising needs to be proportionate to fundraising goals and to reflect an understanding of the organisation's relationship with actual and potential investors. Newer ventures will require a higher investment in fundraising than those with an established and well-nurtured pool of investors.

You will need appropriate, but not excessive, **staffing** levels. Understaffing can erode the organisation's ability to deliver just as overstaffing diverts funds that can best be used for programmes or service delivery.

Seeking people – volunteers, trustees and board members – who represent companies, trusts or foundations and are prepared personally to help the organisation can be key. The quality and standing of the people you bring to the organisation in this way sends out a clear message about who you are and the worth of what you do.

Look for the right kind of patron. Patronage used to carry with it financial obligations, but today this is not always so. Celebrities can be, and often are, used to promote the organisational profile. There is an obvious caveat: stars can fall as well as rise. Sometimes they come down with a crash, and yesterday's heroes can be today's newspaper headlines – on the wrong page.

It remains true, however, that celebrities and high-profile business figures may lend weight and interest to your cause. The golden rule is that whomever you recruit to assist you and whatever their roles (as employees, board members, patrons, or promoters), if they are encouraging others to give, *they must make a financial commitment themselves* as well as be willing to contribute in other ways to the organisation's mission, vision and values.

RAISING THE FUNDS TO SUPPORT YOUR ASPIRATIONS

There are four main questions you should ask:

- Who might choose you? That is, who are your "prospects"?

- Why are they going to choose you? What value would they derive from supporting you?

- What must you do to encourage as many people as possible to choose you?

- How are you going to enable them to give, give again, and increase their support over time?

WHO MIGHT CHOOSE YOU?

Support comes from four sources: grantmaking trusts and foundations, public funding bodies, companies, and individuals.

Grantmaking bodies are *entities that make gifts according to the value system by which they were set up.* They are established by a person, family, group of people, or company. Directories of **grantmaking trusts and foundations** are published regularly in many countries, and information may also be found on the Internet. Many trusts and foundations publish guidelines on their *values (giving*

interests), donation policies, and the timing and form of applications. Once you have ensured that their giving interests match your organisation's work, an application is more likely to be successful if it adheres closely to the guidelines set forth for the application. Building a good relationship with trust and foundation administrators is also an important aspect of success.

Like grantmaking trusts and foundations, **public funding bodies** have guidelines about those areas they support, and the timing and form of applications required from those seeking funding.

Companies can be a useful source of funds and other support. If your organisation's aims fit with a company's articulated social responsibility programme or matches its corporate strategic objectives, an approach to the right person in the organisation is well worthwhile. Where possible, a personal approach is always preferable, but access to the right level of corporate authority is not always easy. Identifying a member of your own board of governors or trustees who might be able to promote your organisation with companies is often the best way to start.

RAISING THE FUNDS TO SUPPORT YOUR ASPIRATIONS

Individuals whom you might want to target need to have the financial ability (capacity) to give as well as the inclination to give. In terms of their inclination to support you, they will fall into four rough categories: those who believe in philanthropy and care about your cause, those who don't but are open to persuasion, those who don't care, and those who are hostile. How you deal with each group obviously will differ, but generally it makes sense to prioritise your activities according to levels of "warmth," devoting more effort to Category One lovers than to Category Four fighters.

It's often assumed that wealthy individuals are under an obligation to give away their money, so there is a natural tendency to concentrate on them as a source of funds. This approach overlooks the fact that not only is philanthropy defined by culture, but it also varies in and between individuals and social structures due to the incentives and pressures peculiar to a particular society. These may be overt, such as tax concessions, or take the form of more subtle social pressures. Wealthy individuals must be part of the strategy; they should be categorised as described above and treated accordingly.

Reviewer's Comment
Research shows that individuals provide more donation income to NPOs than business, government, or trusts and foundations. Also, these individuals often are not wealthy.

WHY PROSPECTS MIGHT CHOOSE YOU: SHARED VALUES
Your case for support is your opportunity to set forth the values that will attract support. It should be based on clarity: clarity of vision, mission, values, and communication. The strength of your case and the quality of your marketing – the ways in which you get your message across – will be the major factors in attracting support. Whether you are approaching major donors or people who give small annual or monthly contributions, donor prospects need to know how your organisation is making a difference and how their engagement can contribute to positive change.

The public profile of your organisation is based largely on its degree of visibility, the kind of people and organisations that fall within its ambit, the quality and consistency of its media positioning, its leadership, and its donors.

Continues on next page

Perceptions of what you do and who supports you are central. Just as profit-making organisations create and rely on brand perception, NPOs should create and communicate clear messages and positive resonance around what they do. Understanding the donor's motivation for giving creates an opportunity to receive.

MOTIVATION TO GIVE

Philanthropy	Self-Interest
• Further the values in which one believes • Contribute and share • Create opportunities • Advance the interests and potential of individuals and society • Acquire power	• Promote personal values • Enjoy giving • Gain respect and recognition • Be part of a community • Provide security • Maintain quality of one's degree, college and university

OPPORTUNITY TO RECEIVE

Creating a profile of your potential supporters and understanding how you might match your organisation's "product" with that profile will enable you to engage prospects appropriately.

Just as your NPO needs an organisational map to take it from where it is to where it wants to be, so you need a "map" or plan for taking investors from where they are to where you want them to be.

WHAT WILL ENABLE PROSPECTS TO INITIATE AND INCREASE THEIR SUPPORT?

This is the "fundraising" element of your operation – how you enable people to act on their values. Your aim is to create a large and growing "platform" of investors in all your stakeholder groups, to retain their confidence and loyalty, and to increase their support. It doesn't matter whether people are giving in their individual capacities or in their roles with trusts and foundations, companies or public bodies. The relationship of the individual to your organisation is of primary significance.

Reviewer's Comment

In relation to businesses, trusts/foundations or public funding agencies, your organisation also needs a sound bilateral relationship at the organisational level to ensure continuity and viability of support as changes in personnel inevitably occur on both sides.

RAISING THE FUNDS TO SUPPORT YOUR ASPIRATIONS

How you find prospects depends on your type of organisation. Educational institutions have alumni, and arts organisations have audiences and prospects identified through friends and membership programmes, events, and mailing lists. Social charities attract interest through the media, events (particularly those involving celebrities), mailing lists and market research.

The donor "pyramid" is used as an illustration of the donation process and how it is driven. The objective is to move investors on to the pyramid at an appropriate level and, through improving your understanding of them and building strong relationships, to grow their support up the donor pyramid. The example opposite shows in general how this might be done, but each organisation must determine how it defines each category.

Research should indicate where each investor fits on the pyramid in terms of ability to give. Building strong relationships aims to increase donor confidence in your programmes and increase donor benefits, to the point where donors maximise their potential to give.

A prospect's potential to give

Willingness to give

= Credibility of your programme

When a prospect's ability to give matches the willingness to give, the programme has been successful. The difference between the two indicates how much work is needed and what resources have to be allocated to reduce the gap.

Amount of Donation:

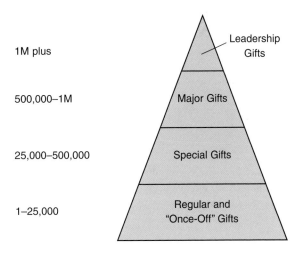

Note: Your organisation's specific circumstances will determine the amount that you consider to be a "leadership," "major" or "special" gift. Whether it is 10,000 or 1,000,000, the principle remains the same.

People generally won't give until they are asked to give (though there are exceptions). If they wish, they can turn down the option, but it is important that they get the chance. "Making the ask" (asking for support) takes many forms. It can be person to person; through direct mail, advertising, networks, volunteer activities or events; or by telephone. The form of the "ask" should reflect the level of relationship. Is the person to whom you're talking a prospect or a donor? If a donor, is he or she one with whom you're building a particular relationship with a particular goal in mind regarding the size of the gift?

Anxieties about "making the ask," particularly in face-to-face situations, can be an obstacle to fundraisers. The anxieties may be about money, or they may arise from cultural issues (for example, if talking about money is inappropriate) or from a fear of rejection. You can overcome the problem by understanding the relationship between gifts and money. Remember, you're not asking for money but for a gift. Money is transformed into the purpose (for which your organisation exists) through the organisation's values (to which you are committed). A fundraiser's most important attribute is that commitment to, and belief in, the organisation's values.

The way in which you frame "the ask" is usually determined by which form of fundraising you are engaged in. Fundraising campaigns can be divided into two types: annual and capital.

Annual campaigns are "bread and butter," repetitive, income-generating activities, designed to maintain a healthy cash flow and ensure delivery on annual strategic objectives. Through these campaigns, organisations identify and attract donors.

Capital campaigns are fixed-term in nature and central to your planning, because capital provision is necessary if the organisation is to deliver on its articulated mission. Capital can be equipment, buildings or endowments (that is, capital investments offering a return to be used for operational costs) or a combination of all three. Capital campaigns should help drive the organisation to a higher level, and enhance its support and prestige among its stakeholders. In the long run, this will benefit annual giving and future capital campaigns.

A thorough feasibility study is central to a successful capital campaign. The study should first examine the organisation's internal preparation, which would include its leadership, the case for support, and its financial and human resources. Secondly, the study should include scrutiny of its external support (issues such as visibility and brand perception, testing the case for support and financial goals with key stakeholders, priority of your campaign against others concurrent with it, and so on). For optimum credibility, a feasibility study should be conducted by an external consultancy, not simply because of the expertise it might bring but also because its advice is more independent and not driven by internal agendas.

Annual and capital campaigns employ the same publicity techniques. The message (which usually frames the case for and makes the "ask") is put across through the organisation's leadership (its annual fund board and/or campaign board); by direct mail, brochures, leaflets and magazines; by electronic media; by means of "telethons"; by personal, prearranged meetings; and through events.

Synchronisation and promotion of capital campaigns with annual activities is a key management issue. It is important to work effectively alongside any tax incentives offered by government. Thoroughly understand the opportunities for tax relief provided by donations and shape your programmes, gifts and targets to maximise these opportunities, in order to both increase revenues and build confidence and credibility with donors.

Legacy/bequest fundraising (different words for gifts at death) is an important and specialised area of fundraising. Unless you are operating in a philanthropic environment where legal structures encourage individuals to make legacies and where both the organisation and the individual receive financial benefits for doing so within a donor's lifetime, the timing of income received from legacies is not predictable. The "counting" of legacy income in annual and capital campaigns needs policy clarification within the organisation and with the individual when negotiating legacies in the context of organisational objectives.

MARKETING YOUR ORGANISATION

There are some basic rules for successful marketing, summed up in the acronym IMPACT developed by Kay Sprinkel Grace and Alan L. Wendroff. The rules are not especially complicated but they are effective, and doing them right will ensure that your organisation is to be noticed by the right people for the right reasons. IMPACT stands for:

Impression: Clarify the impression you're trying to convey.

Message: Be bold, be clear, and focus on the people who are benefiting from what you do. Turn the mirror outward not inward.

Product: Define the benefits of what you do.

Ability: Focus on your track record and accomplishments. Stress your credibility.

Case: Is your case for support communicated effectively, convincingly and powerfully?

Timing: Ensure that your communications are consistent and your solicitations sensitive to the donor's readiness to engage.

You can communicate IMPACT principles through various channels:

- Media (publicity, promotions, advertising, organisational literature) describe your organisation and what you do.

- Events draw people into your programme and generate publicity for investors. Events such as auctions and ticketed dinners can in themselves be fundraisers. Such events need to attract celebrities and key leadership investors.

- Sponsors – companies and individuals – supporting your events or programmes add profile and build brand. Maximising the profile of your event maximises your sponsors' profiles as well.

- Clubs, memberships and friends' programmes create networks of investors who derive benefit from being "in the swim" and who are offered particular rewards for increased participation.

- Patrons (high-profile people and corporations) can add resonance and increase investment.

RELATIONSHIP BUILDING AND STEWARDSHIP

"**B**uild good relationships and profitable transactions will follow" is a guiding principle central to the ability of NPOs to receive support for their work.

The principle that holds together, and drives forward, successful development programmes is stewardship: how you care, and show that you care, for the organisations and people supporting you. Be imaginative and conscientious in the way you mark, evaluate and renew partnership with your supporters.

Start with factors that, while simple, are often the hardest to get right:

- Ensure that data is correct and be meticulous in recording names and contact details accurately.

- Record the first contact, ensure you respond appropriately to that and to subsequent contacts, and note "next steps" for each stage of contact.

- Record and acknowledge stepped upgrades in giving – for example, when a donor who gives a small amount each month gives a larger contribution to a special project.

- Seek to understand what motivates people and organisations to get involved with your organisation, and show your understanding by appropriate communication and action.

- Engage, inform and communicate at every level and stage of the partnership, always stressing the positive (the community arising from the support), not the needs of your organisation.

- Never talk about "costs" and "money"; always talk about "investment" and "gifts."

- Acknowledge the choice the donor is making in supporting your cause.

- Be inventive and consistent in the ways you thank your donors.

CONCLUSION

The professionalism and credibility of nonprofits are key to how well they flourish and meet their objectives.

Stewardship of the people and organisations giving to you is a cornerstone of this process. Respect their support and entrench that respect in all the activities of your organisation and in the values and behaviours of all people who represent you, to ensure they continue to give and to ensure they attract others to do the same.

Making a gift should involve values and care. Receiving a gift needs to recognise and reflect that.

AUTHOR

ADRIENNE HALL

After graduation from Wits University, South Africa, with a BA Honours in languages and music, Adrienne joined a multinational financial services corporation, working in marketing and public relations before becoming Director of Alumni Affairs at Wits University in 1976, a post which she held for six years. She was asked to join The Urban Foundation, a social-action think-tank agency working to dismantle apartheid, as Marketing and Communications Manager, prior to taking up a one-year contract with the London School of Economics in 1984.

She worked independently as a consultant in the UK and South Africa before joining St. Hilda's College, Oxford, as Director of Development and Fellow in 1987. From 1999 to 2004, she was Director of Alumni Affairs and Development at Strathclyde University in Scotland. She now works as an independent consultant in marketing, communications and development as Director of her own company, Beerstecher Hall Consulting.

She has presented at CASE (Council for Advancement and Support of Education) conferences and the Institute of Fund-Raising in the UK, on a particular area of innovation which she has lead in alumni and development programming, that of creating alumni mentor/angel investor networks to support student, faculty and alumni start-up enterprises.

The author would like to thank John Gaunt, mentor, friend and former boss, for his incisive help with the editing of this *Quick*Guide.

Gerlinde Scholz, Reviewer

Gerlinde Scholz is one of the most experienced development professionals working in Australia today. Her career with the University of Melbourne (1990-2004) culminated in her appointment as the University's first Director of Development in 1999.

Gerlinde has contributed to the development of her profession as an author, editor, reviewer, speaker and mentor. She served on the executive board of the Association of Development and Alumni Professionals in Education (ADAPE) in Australia at state and federal levels throughout the 1990s, including a term as President of ADAPE Victoria/Tasmania, and as editor of the Association's national magazine Face-To-Face from 1998 to 1999. Gerlinde is a fellow of ADAPE, has been a longstanding member of CASE (Council for Advancement and Support of Education), and has presented papers at national and international conferences for both of these professional organisations.

Gerlinde is originally from Germany. She settled in Melbourne, Australia, in 1984 after having lived in Canada for 18 months. She holds a Master's degree in History and an Honours degree in Latin American Studies, and speaks Spanish and German.